DON'T ASSUME!

Some characteristics were assigned to animals more or less by mistake. All it takes is one look and reality can appear in quite a different light. Ostriches stick their heads in the sand, you say? Not at all. What, do you think that opossums spent the whole day hanging from tree branches by their tail? The young can manage it for a while, but adults use their tail to maintain balance on short branches. ▸

Oppossum hanging by its tail

WHAT OUR ANCESTORS BELIEVED

Distorted ideas about animals can have a long tradition. For example, some of our ancestors believed that when an owl, especially a little owl, hoots, it ushers in danger. Who doesn't get a fright at night, right? However, there's no reason to believe these superstitions as they mostly don't have even a kernel of truth in them. ◂

DON'T BELIEVE EVERYTHING YOU SEE

You've certainly read a fairy tale or seen a movie that showed certain animals as evil creatures. Let's take the wolf, for example! He threatened not only Little Red Riding Hood but the three little pigs as well! What we need to realize, though, is that such a depiction and reality may be miles apart. ▾

PEOPLE WERE AFRAID OF THEM

Very often, people used to associate certain animals, such as bats and black cats, with dark forces. Naturally, this caused fear. These animals were considered to be helpers of witches, vampires, and many forces of evil. Fear of such animals is ingrained so deep that some people are afraid of them to this very day. That is a pity, because these are some very interesting creatures that definitely don't deserve the bad reputation they have. ▸

Myth №1

BAT

BLOODTHIRSTY VAMPIRE

Bloodthirsty vampires. Flying mice. Disease carriers. Signs of evil. That's what usually comes to mind when someone mentions bats. But what if those things aren't entirely true? Let's take a closer look at these critters. Surely you'll realize soon that there's nothing to be afraid of.

BATS ARE BLIND

Bats have tiny eyes but are by no means blind. For example, fruit bats–a large type of bat–use sight to maintain their orientation while flying. Furthermore, bats are equipped with echolocation–they send out invisible waves. These reflect from subjects ahead and return to the bats. The echo lets bats know there's an obstacle in front of them and allows them to avoid it in a blink of an eye. Or eat it, if they're so inclined. ▼

BATS TANGLE IN PEOPLE'S HAIR

People used to believe that bats will tangle into a woman's long hair if the woman has a guilty conscience. They then lead the person to a witch or demon. However, this is just a folk tale. Thanks to their ultrasound, bats can recognize such small obstacles that it's impossible for them to get tangled in anyone's hair. On the contrary, you can be sure they'll give you a wide berth. ▲

BATS SUCK PEOPLE'S BLOOD

People imagine bats as bloodthirsty creatures that suck their blood. It's true that a certain kind of bat lives off blood. However, it poses little harm to humans as it has a soft spot for animal blood. You can now sleep more peacefully, knowing that there are only three bat species that do this, out of more than 1,300 that inhabit Earth. Furthermore, they can be encountered only in South and Central America. ▼

BAT = A SIGN OF EVIL

In many cultures, bats are considered a sign of evil and associated with witches, demons, and other forces. This is mainly because bats are nocturnal animals and people have always been afraid of the dark. However in some countries, such as China, they're viewed as a symbol of luck. In fact, the character used to name them–fu–is the same as the one that denotes luck. ▲

BATS ARE PESTS

Bats are immensely useful animals. They fly and hunt at night when most other creatures are deeply asleep. Well, there are some exceptions, like annoying, buzzing mosquitoes. Most bats catch pesky insects and other pests. Certain tropical bats even pollinate flowers and allow you to enjoy avocados, mangoes, or bananas. That's why it's important to protect them. ▼

BATS ARE FLYING MICE

Wrong! Bats are the only mammals that can fly; they have very little in common with mice. Their membranous wings enable them to fly quickly and deftly. Because the wings are flexible, bats not only can perform various maneuvers and quickly swerve while flying, but also reverse! ▲

Myth №2

BEAR

TERROR TO THE WOODS

Dangerous and aggressive furballs. Carnivores who like to have humans for dinner. Unpredictable under any circumstances. Sleepers who snore through the winter. Do you think all of this applies to bears? Let's take a closer look at them.

BEWARE! A BEAR!

As if bears had no better job than to chase poor tourists around! They're shy, and once they smell a human, their preferred reaction is to hide. If you do encounter a bear, don't let its body language confuse you: if a bear gets on its hind legs, it doesn't want to attack you. It simply has a superior view that way and is able to catch scents better then when it's on all fours. Of course, it pays to be careful and not provoke bears needlessly. ►

IF THERE'S A BEAR AT YOUR HEELS, CLIMB A TREE

A hasty escape up a tree won't help you much when you're dealing with a bear. For example, the American black bear or grizzly can climb better than many mountain climbers! Instead, keep calm and slowly retreat from the place where you encountered the animal. It's also good to speak in a deep, unexcited voice so that the bear realizes you're a human. Once that happens, it will likely leave immediately. ◄

BEARS ARE DEEPLY ASLEEP THROUGHOUT THE WINTER

Bears do hibernate over winter, but it's not like they set their alarm clock to "spring" and spend the entire winter in bed. When autumn arrives, they eat a lot, fatten up, find a lair, and lay down to sleep. Their life processes are the same as in summer, though; bears simply lower their body temperature by a couple of degrees. They even sense things that go on around them and can wake up at any time during the winter, get something to eat, and then turn in again. If the winter is mild, they may not go to sleep at all. ▼

BEARS AREN'T GOOD RUNNERS

Running from a bear doesn't pay off–that's because the animal can run faster than humans and would catch up with you in a split second. It's as fast as a horse and additionally quite a tireless runner. All you need to do is adhere to fundamental rules, not provoke bears, and not be afraid of their presence beforehand. ▲

BEARS LIKE THE TASTE OF HONEY

You've certainly noticed that bears have a sweet tooth for honey in many fairy tales. But is it the only thing bears eat? Not by a long shot. They like to eat honey, but they gobble it up with all the bees and larvae that are inside the honeycomb too. Bears are omnivores, which means they eat other things apart from meat: grass, roots, and various berries. ▶

BEARS HAVE BAD EYESIGHT

Bears definitely don't need to get glasses; their eyesight isn't as bad as is generally said. They see, at the very least, as well as humans. Their eyes work well at night too. Apart from that, bears can rely on their perfect sense of smell; they can perceive scents from up to a 4.3-mile distance! ◀

Myth №3

FOX

SLY LITTLE CRITTER

A wicked rogue who outsmarts just about everybody. A cunning, sly wood critter that uses clever tricks to get anything it wants. A terror to be reckoned with. Foxes are so known for their smarts that sly people are even compared to them. Are they really so wily as everybody seems to think? What does its foxiness even consist of?

CUTE FOX CUBS CAN BE HOUSEHOLD PETS

Look at these two spry little devils! They look quite cute, which is why some people believe they'd make nice pets. Sadly, as foxes grow up, they start to be more and more fearful of humans and could attack them in self-defense. It's better to avoid bothering them; they're wild animals and as such belong in the wild. ▼

Cute little cubs

WILY LITTLE THIEVES

Foxes really aren't picky and feed on many different things. They have a reputation as pests in many places because they dare to attack animals in chicken coops or pens. It's no surprise, considering that these obstacles pose little challenge to their dexterity. However, it's not their habit to go thieving on purpose. ▲

FOXES ARE DANGEROUS

People were afraid of foxes from time immemorial because foxes caused harm to them: they killed chickens and other farm critters, which is something that farmers naturally didn't like. That's why these animals started to be depicted as cruel predators not to be trusted. It's important to take into account that a fox is a wild animal and acts with accordance to its natural instincts. ▾

CUNNING FOXES

In many stories, foxes appear as smart creatures that shrewdly hunt down anything they want. One such story, the Fox and the Crow, can be found in Aesop's fables. Other stories even assign them magic powers. Some have more or less favorable opinions on foxes. Let's hope we manage to improve this reputation! ▴

SLY AS A FOX

Compared to other animals, foxes don't have above-average intelligence. Rather, their smarts consist of caution and wariness. They are very hard to catch because their sensitive noses can quickly and accurately recognize traps. If a fox senses danger, it prefers to seek a hiding place. It's always on its guard! ▾

FOXES ARE LONERS

Pictures often show a solitary fox, be it in the forest or on the hunt. It's true that, unlike other predators, foxes usually don't hunt in packs. Nevertheless, they're not solitary; a fox typically finds a lifelong partner and takes turns looking after the young. ▴

OSTRICH

FEATHERED COWARD

A coward, a shrinking violet, or simply someone who wants to avoid problems by taking the easiest route available? Or is it just stupid enough to stick its head in the sand for no reason at all? Can ostriches even be deemed birds if they can't fly? Let's collectively find out if there's at least a kernel of truth in these claims.

OSTRICHES STICK THEIR HEAD IN THE SAND

Do ostriches stick their head in the sand when they feel threatened? That's just a myth. If they did this, they'd be unable to breathe. How is it, then, that this superstition came to be? When an ostrich is in danger, it crouches down and places its long neck on the ground. This is sort of a camouflage . It works so well that from a distance it looks like the ostrich has its head stuck under the ground. ▸

OSTRICHES ARE STUPID

Ostriches have a small brain, approximately walnut sized. This means that an ostrich's brain is smaller than its eye! OK, so these birds aren't exactly geniuses, but they're not completely stupid either. Otherwise they'd be unable to protect themselves and their young from predators. ◂

IF YOU HAVE FEATHERS, YOU CAN FLY

Even though the ostrich is a winged bird, it can't fly. Nonetheless, its wings aren't just for show! Ostriches can run like the wind and while they do so, their wings help them balance their body. Similarly, peacocks flaunt their feathers when courting a mate or when trying to drive away an unwanted visitor. ▼

WHAT DO OSTRICHES HAVE IN COMMON WITH CAMELS?

Because ostriches originated in Africa where they inhabit savannas and desert areas, they're well adapted to living in the local climate. They even used to be called "camel birds," not only due to a certain similarity between the two of them, but mainly because they are able to withstand high temperatures and survive several days without water, just like camels. ▲

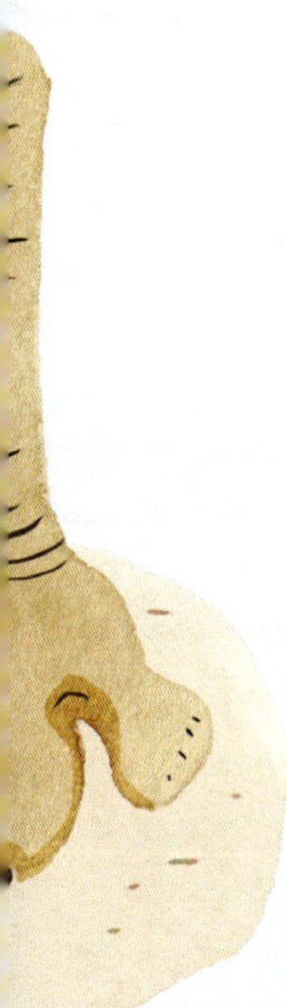

OSTRICHES ARE COWARDLY

Calling an ostrich a coward might not pay off. In fact, everybody should be wary of them! The truth is that ostriches have really strong, long legs they can use to give anybody quite a kick. Even lions can end up on the receiving end of a proper kicking! ◀

TAKE A LOOK & THERE'S YOUR ANSWER

Owing to the head-in-the-sand superstition, a lot of people believe that ostriches don't look around much. Quite the contrary, in fact! Being the largest bird species of all, ostriches have a pretty good view of their surroundings, especially due to their long neck and great height. They also have excellent eyesight and the largest eyes out of all terrestrial animals. ▲

Myth №5

HYENA

LAUGHING GOOD-FOR-NOTHING

Cowardly thieves who rob predators of their prey. Stupid and ugly animals that don't really help anybody. Scavengers who wickedly scoff at everybody. In Africa, their home, these animals were even accused of consorting with witches. But is there any truth to this?

HYENAS ARE STUPID

This conclusion doesn't fit hyenas at all. In fact, they're very smart and can crack various puzzles–how to get to hidden food, for example. Hyenas can estimate the number of approaching enemies and evaluate whether they can overpower them or not. In many cases, hyenas are smarter then chimpanzees and are able to learn from one another, passing their experiences down the line. ◂

Fearless creature

COWARDLY COWARDS DOING COWARDLY THINGS

People often consider hyenas cowardly–maybe it's their appearance. A hyena's hind legs are shorter than its forelegs, making it look like it crouches, like it's afraid of something. But hyenas are pretty fearless, actually, and dare to attack even lions. ▸

HYENAS ARE RELATED TO DOGS

Although these predators are similar to canines, they're not related. Hyenas constitute a separate family: Hyaenidae. They differ from dogs in anatomy, lifestyle, and homeland. After all, not every little dog can frolic around African savannas and chase prey along the way. ▼

THIEVES & SCAVENGERS

We're not going to claim that hyenas have never enjoyed a carcass for dinner. What isn't true is that they don't hunt at all! In fact, they're very competent hunters. People accuse them of thievery because they often see them fight lions for a piece of meat. But it's quite the other way around. Lions frequently attempt to relieve hyenas of their main meal. ▲

THEY'RE GOOD FOR NOTHING

You think that hyenas aren't useful at all? Well, that's just a load of nonsense. Hyenas perform a vital function in the environment they inhabit–not only do they maintain a natural balance, purity, and health, but they also may affect our human lives. They can live in peace alongside us if we give them the chance. ▼

HYENAS LAUGH ALL THE TIME

At some point, you've surely seen a TV program in which a hyena laughs like it's lost its mind. You want to know what they find so funny? The sounds they emit only resemble laughter; in fact, this is their way of talking to each other. Different sounds have different meanings–greeting, celebration, or warning. ▲

Myth №6

PIG

DIRTY LAZYBONES

You stink like a pig. You sweat like a pig. You're lazy like a pig. You're surely aware that this is what some people say. But are pigs truly so dirty, stinky, and lazy? Are they smart or stupid? We'll try to clarify what's really going on with pigs.

YOU STINK LIKE A PIG

Have you ever heard the saying "you stink like a pig" or "you sweat like a pig"? Well, stop saying that because it's nothing but nonsense. Pigs don't have sweat glands, so they're unable to sweat. Furthermore, they're very clean; for example, they relieve themselves at one spot and one spot only. ▼

ALL PIGS ARE PINK

Just take a look and see how much individual pigs can differ from one another. Domestic pigs may be pink, but also piebald or reddish. Their body structure, ears, and other things can also be quite diverse–it depends on the breed. And then there are the wild relatives of pigs, boars, who have substantially longer bristles in order to survive when there's bitter cold outside. ▲

PIGS ARE DIRTY

Many people assume that pigs are slobs, perhaps because pigs like to roll around in mud when given the opportunity. The thing is that they do so for practical reasons, to protect themselves from the sun and tiresome insects and to cool down. They can't just apply a skin cream like us humans, you know! ►

DUMB CREATURES

In case you didn't know this, pigs are the smartest animals you can find at the farmyard. They can be trained just like dogs. Pigs are very smart, which is why they need to be active or playing all the time in order to entertain themselves. It's said that their ways of thinking and dealing with problems can be compared to those of a three-year old child. ◄

GOOD FOR NOTHING BUT FOOD

People have noticed how intelligent pigs are and therefore use them for many things. In France, the excellent sense of smell pigs have is used for finding the delicious truffles that grow underground. Some people keep miniature pigs as pets. ►

CHUBBY LAYABOUTS

People feed animals to fatten them up nicely. Even though the pig is no lightweight, breaking into a run poses no problem for it. Domestic pigs can reach a top speed of 12.4 mph, while boars are able to run at 31 to 37.3 mph. That's the usual speed of people driving a car in a city! ◄

Myth №7

RAT

THIEF FROM THE SEWERS

Dirty, overgrown creeps that live in sewers. Pests that aren't afraid of stealing food or trash in order to have something to eat. Carriers of diseases, even the plague. Creatures with a disgusting tail. Are all rats like that? And what about sewer rats? Let's look closely at them and properly check things out.

RATS CAN GROW TO BE AS BIG AS CATS

In some parts of the world, like in the remote rain forests of Papua New Guinea, rats can grow to be rather big. But not as big as a cat! Cats weigh somewhere between 3.7 to 9.9 pounds, whereas this whopper has a weight of approximately 3.3 pounds. The rats we usually encounter generally weigh about 1.1 to 2.2 pounds. ◂

RATS = DISEASE CARRIERS

In the past, people believed that rats carry diseases. In the middle of the 14th century, Europe experienced an epidemic outbreak of plague known as the Black Death, a disease which afflicted many patients. Rats were immediately condemned as its originators. That's only partially true–the guilt rested with fleas carrying the bacteria that cause plague. And even then, it might not have been rats that brought fleas to Europe in the first place ... ◂

RATS ARE DIRTY

People have come to the conclusion that if rats live in the sewers, they must be dirty. However, even wild rats take great care to keep themselves clean. Overall, they're very clean animals and groom themselves several times a day, just like cats. If they can't reach a place on their body, a willing buddy helps them out. ▸

THEIR TAILS ARE UNPLEASANT TO THE TOUCH

People mind a rat or sewer rat's tail, you say? Well, such a tail might not be appealing to look at, but when it comes to touching, it's far from unpleasant. To the touch, a rat tail is quite similar to human skin and has a great value to the rodents as it helps them maintain body temperature and keep balance while they're climbing. ◂

RATS BRING NO BENEFIT TO US

Quite the opposite! Rats can be helpful to people and even save their lives! There are certain special organizations that managed to notice how smart rats are and trained them to search for mines in Africa. Doctors and scientists often make use of them as well. ▸

RATS FROM THE SEWERS ARE THE SAME THING AS PET RATS

When a person keeps a pet rat at home, some visitors are shocked when they find out. Yuck, a rat! But a domesticated rat differs quite a lot from its wild relatives. It's a very clean animal, immensely intelligent, curious, and playful. It loves its owners and likes to cuddle with them. ▴

Myth №8

WOLF

DANGEROUS LONER

Dangerous creatures that have no place in nature. Bloodthirsty beasts that dare attack farm animals and even people. Not particularly intelligent. Solitary animals howling at the moon. Well, poor wolves will certainly not brag about this. Have a quick look at whether people are right to assign all these qualities to them.

BIG BAD WOLF

Little Red Riding Hood. Three little pigs. Werewolves. What do they have in common? The alleged bad guy, the big bad wolf. However, such a portrayal is pretty skewed and affected by long-standing prejudice. A wolf is a very shy creature and would definitely never strike up a chat with a human. Stories of this kind take the intelligence and ingrained talent for hunting in packs that wolves naturally exhibit and twist them into an attempt to trick their prey and hunt it down. ▼

AGE-OLD ENEMIES

Did you know that wolves are the ancestors of dogs? The qualities that dogs have and people appreciate are derived from the qualities of wolves. Both wolves and dogs have sharp senses, are quick to learn, and can establish relationships with their peers and cooperate with them. Long ago, wolves even behaved in a friendly manner if they encountered a person for the first time. The enmity probably began only after wolves started to attack shepherds' herds in a time of need. ▲

THERE'S A LOT OF WOLVES IN THE WORLD

You can find wolves at many places around the planet, true, but there's definitely no abundance of them. Quite on the contrary, this species is considered endangered worldwide. Humans don't really help much, as they kill wolves off in many countries. Fortunately, it seems like the total numbers are starting to rise again and wolves are beginning to return even to those areas where there's long been no sign of them. ◂

BLOODTHIRSTY CREATURE

Are you afraid that you might be attacked by a wolf when you're in the wild? That's extremely unlikely. Wolves are so shy that even scientists find it difficult to find opportunities to observe them in their natural environment. So rest assured, they're certainly not waiting behind the nearest tree to get you. ▾

PREDATORS THROUGH & THROUGH

Yeah, we're in agreement on that one– wolves truly are outstanding predators. They've adapted in every way possible to live under the harshest conditions. All they need to survive is a food source and a place to hide their newborn young. However, wolves never purposefully attack human residences unless they're in great need. ◂

WOLF THE LONER

Are wolves truly loners? Well, they can be, but their family and pack always come first. Wolves have an elaborate system to communicate with one another– they lick each other, rub shoulders, or howl. Apart from that, they're very sensitive and take care not only of their families but also other wounded wolves. ◂

Myth №9

SNAKE

SLIMY DANGER

Evil, poisonous creatures that attack other animals or even humans without issuing any warning. Their skin is slimy, unpleasant to the touch. They're said to be deaf, so you must shout loudly to get them to leave you alone. And what does their body even look like-aren't they just a head with an extremely long tail? Join us to find out!

Smallest snake

Grass snake

Anaconda

ALL SNAKES ARE POISONOUS

Snakes vary quite a lot–in body size, coloration, or hunting style. One thing is certain, though–not all of them are poisonous. There are over 3,000 snake species living on Earth but only some of them are poisonous. Even though you need to beware the poisonous and huge kinds, many other can be kept at home in terrariums with no issue whatsoever. ▲

SNAKES ARE SLIMY

Most of the time, people don't exactly line up to touch a snake. But why is that? A lot of folks believe that snakes are slimy to the touch. Quite the contrary! Just muster up your courage, and you'll immediately find out that snakes aren't slimy at all, not even a little bit. Actually, their skin is dry, scaly, and wonderfully smooth to the touch. ▶

SNAKES ARE EVIL, VENGEFUL CREATURES

Do you believe that snakes attack people on purpose? That they hide in the grass, poised to attack? Far from it! Most snakes prefer to slither away from humans rather than approach them. They're definitely not planning how best to hunt us down, and they attack only when scared or provoked. ►

SNAKES CAN HYPNOTIZE THEIR PREY

There must have been a time when you noticed how fixed a snake's gaze can be. Don't worry; the reptile isn't trying to hypnotize you! Snakes don't have eyelids, which means that they're unable to blink. Puzzle solved! In actuality, they catch prey in completely different ways. ◄

AS DEAF AS A POST

Have you ever seen someone playing a pipe while a cobra moves to the sound of the music? Then it must have occurred to you that snakes might have quite good hearing. But snakes have no ears and thus can't perceive sounds. However, they possess an inner organ that allows them to feel vibrations. It gives them an outstanding sense of orientation, just like our own ears do. It's in fact the movement of the pipe to which the cobra reacts, not the sound of the instrument. ►

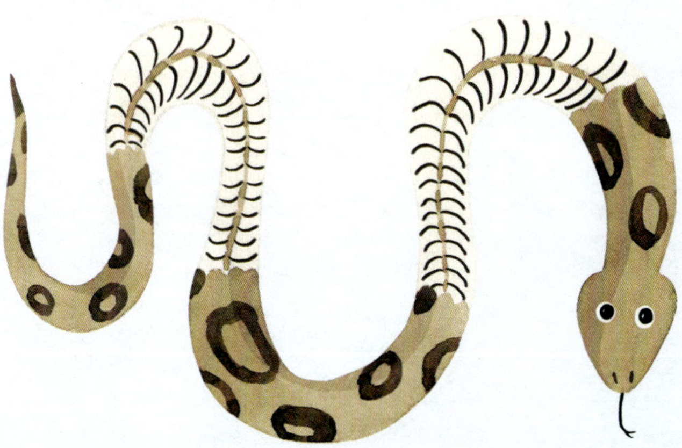

SNAKE BODY IS JUST A HUGE TAIL

If snakes consisted only of a tail and head, it'd be pretty hard for them to move. In reality, there's of course a thin, legless body between these two points that allows the snake to move by pushing off the ground. The tail starts where ribs end. ◄

Myth №10

SHARK

TERROR TO THE SEAS

The terror of the seas, respected by all fish. A man-eater who turns swimmers into little snacks. There's no shark that would defy this description: all of them are vengeful carnivores, with no exceptions. They're clumsy hunters whose success is more often than not the result of chance. Such things may flash through people's minds when they hear the word "shark". But are they correct?

TERROR OF THE SEAS

Sharks are, no doubt, majestic beasts that swim around the world's seas and oceans. Most sharks are impressive in length, which earns the respect of any fish or other submarine creatures. After all, who would provoke them, considering that being an irreverent rascal might get you landed on a dinner plate? ▸

GREAT WHITE SHARKS

The great white shark has the worst reputation with people imaginable. It hunts whales, octopuses, turtles, and sometimes penguins. It's a great hunter but rarely subjects humans to its art. How is it, then, that it gained such a bad reputation? A big part of the blame can be laid at the feet of the movies that depict the great white as a man-eater. ◂

ALL SHARKS ARE THE SAME

Just like individual people are different, there are a number of shark species. Some sharks are small, others huge. Some eat meat, yet others feed on plankton. Even the shape of their bodies can vary immensely. Just take a look! ◂

HUMANS AS A QUICK BITE

The great white shark is responsible for some attacks on humans. Even ancient sailors considered it to be a man-eater and tried to get rid of it. In fact, sharks don't hunt people on purpose; it's more likely by accident. There are only about 1.5 lethal shark attacks a year! ▾

CLUMSY HUNTER

Even though it might not seem like it at first glance, sharks are excellent hunters. They can reach high speeds similar to the speed of a passenger car in a city and capture prey by quickly lunging from underneath the surface. Their fantastic sense of smell allows them to catch a whiff of a single drop of blood in 1.2 million gallons of water! What an admirable feat! ◂

THE BIGGEST THREAT TO SHARKS

Do you know what the largest terror to sharks is? If you guessed killer whales, you're partially right. But what really poses the largest threat to sharks is humans. People have been hunting sharks for centuries, be it for their fins or simply because we don't like them. It's possible, though, that sharks might soon face extinction. So do your best to improve their reputation! ◂

Myth №11

TURTLE

CALM SLOWPOKE

Slow in body, slow in spirit. Patient but somewhat boring animals that are never rushing. Have you ever heard the saying "as slow as a turtle"? And what about "crying as hard as a turtle"? Are these idioms even correct? Let's find out together.

AS SLOW AS A TURTLE

It's true that turtles aren't exactly the fastest runners on Earth. They spend most of their days asleep, and if they manage to be awake for a little while, there's certainly no rushing. Typically, turtles are slow and careful, but they can be persuaded to reach considerable speeds if there's a good reason for it. ▸

TURTLES ARE SLOW THINKERS TOO

Now isn't that a colossal mistake! In fact, some turtles are quite smart. You don't believe us? Well, imagine this: turtles can learn from other turtles with whom they share an elaborate system of communication. They are even able to remember places they've visited before! How else to explain that they recall the beach where they were born? ◂

YOU LIVE A NEW LIFE FOR EVERY RING YOU HAVE ON YOUR SHELL

Can a turtle's age be figured out by looking at the "growth ring" on the shell, like it was a tree? Possibly during the first two years of age. But what about the next hundred or more years? That's right–turtles can live to be as old as 150 years, and unless somebody was there to record their precise date of birth, there's no way to know their precise age. ▸

TURTLES ARE GREAT PARENTS

Parental skills of sea turtles are quite different when compared to the way people raise their own young. Turtle females go to the beach where they were born and lay eggs into a hole they dug with their own fins. Then, they bury the eggs and return back to the sea. The little turtles hatch after two months, already able to swim and get their own food. Infallibly, they head right into the sea. ◂

CRYING TURTLES

Turtles cry, that's true. But unlike us humans, their crying is not associated with emotions like sadness. Sea turtles live in seas and therefore drink seawater. They have special ducts in their body that excrete salt. Turtles push the salt out via their eyes, along with tears, so they look like us when we cry. ▸

Turtle "tears"

TURTLES DON'T LIKE COMPANY

When people saw how quickly turtles can withdraw inside their shell, they came to the conclusion that these are not social animals. This, however, is a defense reaction. In fact, it's usual for several individual turtles to live together like a large happy family. ◂

Myth №12

ELEPHANT

TIMID GIANT

Ponderous giants, afraid of the tiniest creatures! On the other hand, those who have an elephant's memory remember quite a lot! The imposing body of an elephant boasts many peculiarities. Do they use their trunk as a straw to drink water? And can you make their day by giving them a peanut? Well, read on and find out.

ELEPHANTS ARE AFRAID OF MICE

When did the myth come to be? Probably as early as ancient Rome, when one thinker recorded this fable in his book, saying that elephants are afraid of mice because these little rodents might crawl inside their trunk. The truth is, however, that if that were to happen, the elephant would just blow the offending creature out. Elephants may avoid mice, but there's no real proof indicating they're truly scared of them. ◂

ELEPHANT MEMORY

It's said that elephants have a fantastic memory. And it's true! They remember the paths they took, even places where they found food and water in the past. They can recognize not only their friends but also enemies. Elephants have the largest brain among all terrestrial mammals, which earns them the right to be included among the smartest animals on Earth. ▸

TRUNK = STRAW

Do you know how elephants drink water? Did you believe that they use their trunk as a straw and simply suck the water in? Far from it! Yes, they do suck the water into their trunk, but immediately after that, they squirt it out, right into their mouth! Elephants use the same method to refresh themselves on hot days–they just use their trunk as a shower. ▲

BIG AND AWKWARD

African elephants are the largest terrestrial mammals on Earth. You might find them clumsy, but in fact they're able to run at a speed of 25 mph. And they can do it almost without making a sound! Additionally, when elephants feel hot, they use their large ears as fans. ◀

PEANUTS! WHAT AN ELEPHANT TREAT

You've certainly seen at least one movie where an elephant gorges on peanuts. But do they eat peanuts in the wild as well? Absolutely not. It'd be hard to get them in African savannas. Elephants prefer to munch on leaves or other plants. They consume over 441 pounds of food each day; that'd make a huge pile of peanuts! ▲

TUSKS ARE JUST LIKE HUMAN TEETH

Elephant tusks are elongated incisors that grow for the entirety of the individual's life and can be as long as 11.5 feet! Unlike human teeth, though, they never fall out or grow back. The tusks are greatly valued by poachers who aren't ashamed to hurt elephants in order to get this precious commodity. Few elephants survive such an encounter. This is why humans pose the greatest threat to them. Let's try to help them–they're on the verge of extinction! ▶

Myth №13

CHAMELEON

MASTER OF DISGUISE

Chameleons would make fantastic spies, seeing as they can change color based on their surroundings and thus blend in perfectly. They're not much different from other reptiles in the remaining respects. Chameleons are slow, clumsy hunters who are unable to hear. Do they really all look the same? Read on and find out.

CHAMELEON, THE MASTER OF DISGUISE

Chameleons change color for many reasons: ambient temperature, their mood, communication with others, or courting a potential mate. Not all of them can display all colors of the rainbow; most chameleon species have only a few basic colors in their repertoire. Their ability to change color is based on special cells in their skin. ▼

Jackson's chameleon

Brookesia micra

Panther chameleons have many colors

ALL CHAMELEONS ARE THE SAME

Did you think that there's only one kind of chameleon? Far from it! There are over 150 chameleon species in the world! Some of them are tiny, not even 0.8 inches long; others are almost as large as a cat. They vary not only in size but also in appearance and coloration. ▲

CHAMELEONS ARE JUST ORDINARY LIZARDS

Oh, come on! There are many things that differentiate chameleons from other reptiles: for example, their bulging eyes that can move independently of each other. This allows the animal to look ahead and aside at the same time. Isn't that cool? Chameleons can use their twining tail to hold onto things and maintain balance while they're moving. Their toes are bound into groups of two or three, forming a suction pad that enables them to firmly grip a branch. ►

SLOW, CLUMSY HUNTERS

Chameleons do move at a rather slow pace, but they're quite known for their hunting skills. That's because chameleons have an incredibly long and fast tongue than moves at more than 16 feet per second. They can stretch it so far that it's twice as long as their body. How's that for hunting? ◄

CHAMELEONS LIVE ONLY IN RAIN FORESTS

It's true that most chameleons can be found in rain forests. However, that doesn't mean you can't encounter them in a desert, semi-desert, or savanna. It's possible to keep them at home in a terrarium as well, but you need to have a great deal of knowledge and provide diligent care! ►

AS DEAF AS A POST

A chameleon's ears aren't visible. Does that necessarily mean that it's completely deaf? Not quite, but its hearing definitely isn't the best. Despite this, chameleons are able to catch certain sound frequencies and vibrations. In their case, sounds are sensed rather than actually heard. ◄

Myth №14

BLACK CAT

BAD LUCK ON LEGS

An animal that is feared because it brings nothing but bad luck. A consort to witches and dark or evil forces. A symbol of evil but also of Halloween. Is it really true that nobody's interested in caring for these cats? Are these black beauties truly veiled in misfortune?

ILL REPUTATION FROM TIME IMMEMORIAL

If you guessed that black cats have always been disliked, you're wrong. Ancient Egyptians, for example, used to revere them! If such a pet died, the owners would have it mummified and mourn for it. ▸

BLACK CATS BRING BAD LUCK

If a cat crosses a person's path, it's considered a bad omen in many countries. Despite this, there are some regions where black cats symbolize luck and prosperity. This attitude is found sometimes in countries such as Scotland, Japan, or Russia. Let's follow their example! ◂

SYMBOL OF EVIL

Black cats have had an ill reputation since the time of legends. The Salem witch trials in colonial America didn't help, either. And let's not forget that if a person encounters a black cat at night, the only thing they see are its glowing eyes. Admittedly, the jumpier among us might find this a bit frightening. ►

WITCH'S RIGHT HAND

Why are black cats associated with witches? A legend which originated in the middle of the 16th century is probably to blame. In this tale, a father and a son set out to travel at night and a black cat crossed their path. They chased it away with stones and the pitiful creature found its way into a house of an alleged witch. When the men encountered this woman, they saw her all beaten up; almost as if she had been hit by stones. People therefore came to the conclusion that witches turn into cats at night and freely roam the countryside. ◄

NOBODY WANTS BLACK CATS

According to a certain study, people usually don't want to adopt a shelter cat if it's black. But this is no longer valid; many people don't allow prejudice to blind them anymore. Black cats even have their own holiday in some places, on November 17. ▼

PREJUDICES ASIDE

Let's sum things up: black cats aren't evil or spooky, nor do they bring ill luck. In fact, they're incredibly intelligent, playful creatures, and if their masters pay proper attention to them, they reward them with unreserved love! ▲

Published in 2022 by Windmill Books,
an Imprint of Rosen Publishing
29 East 21st Street, New York, NY 10010

Author: Pavla Hanáčková
Illustrator: Linh Dao
www.albatrosmedia.eu

Cataloging-in-Publication Data

Names: Dao, Linh. | Hanáčková, Pavla.
Title: Is what they tell us true? / by Linh Dao and Pavla Hanáčková.
Description: New York : Windmill Books, 2022. | Series: Amazing nature
Identifiers: ISBN 9781499487589 (pbk.) | ISBN 9781499487602 (library bound) | ISBN 9781499487596 (6 pack) | ISBN 9781499487619 (ebook)
Subjects: LCSH: Animals--Miscellanea--Juvenile literature.
Classification: LCC QL49.H363 2022 | DDC 590--dc23

Printed in the United States of America

CPSIA Compliance Information: Batch BSWM22: For Further Information contact Rosen Publishing, New York, New York at 1-800-237-9932